D1541235

When Will I Get In?

Sean Price

Raintree

Chicago, Illinois

Designed by Michelle Lisseter, Kim Miracle, and Bigtop
Printed in China

11 10 09 08
10 9 8 7 6 5 4 3 2

Library of Congress
Cataloging-in-Publication Data
Price, Sean.
  When will I get in? : segregation and civil rights / Sean Price.
      p. cm. -- (American history through primary sources)
  Includes bibliographical references and index.
  ISBN 1-4109-2414-9 (hc) -- ISBN 1-4109-2425-4 (pb)
  1. African Americans--Civil rights--History--20th century--Juvenile
literature. 2. African Americans--Segregation--History--Juvenile
literature. 3. United States--Race relations--Juvenile literature. I.
Title. II. Series.
  E185.61.P757 2007
   305.896'073--dc22
                                        2006008485

13-digit ISBNs
978-1-4109-2414-8 (hardcover)
978-1-4109-2425-4 (paperback)

Acknowledgments
The author and publisher are grateful to the following for permission to reproduce copyright material: Bettmann/Corbis **pp. 6**, **15**, **17**, **20**, **23**, **25**; Corbis **pp. 27** (Flip Schulke), **7**, **28–29**; Library of Congress Geography and Map Division **p. 4**; Library of Congress Prints and Photographs Division **pp. 5**, **8**, **9**, **10**, **11**, **13**, **14**, **19**, **21**.

Cover photograph of Elizabeth Eckford, one of the nine black students who gained admission to Little Rock's Central High School, reproduced with permission of Bettman/Corbis.

Photo research by Tracy Cummins.

The publishers would like to thank Nancy Harris and Joy Rogers for their assistance in the preparation of this book.

Every effort has been made to contact copyright holders of any material reproduced in this book. Any omissions will be rectified in subsequent printings if notice is given to the publishers.

Disclaimer

Contents

Some words are printed in bold, **like this**. You can find out what they mean on page 30. You can also look in the box at the bottom of the page where they first appear.

Leaving Slavery Behind

Blacks first came to the United States from Africa. They were brought as **slaves**. Slaves are people who are owned by another person.

As slaves, blacks had no freedom. Many were beaten. Most worked on large farms. These were called **plantations**. Slaves picked crops. They pulled cotton. In the early 1800s, things changed. **Slavery** (owning slaves) was forbidden in the northern United States. But slavery became stronger in the southern United States.

The green and ▶ yellow parts of this map show the states that owned slaves. The states in red were free.

4

civil war	fight between people from the same country
plantation	large farm
slave	person owned by another person
slavery	practice of buying and selling slaves

Slavery ended after the U.S. **Civil War**. A civil war is a fight between people within the same country. The U.S. Civil War lasted from 1861 to 1865. During the war, northern and southern states fought each other. One of their biggest fights was over the issue of slavery.

▼Blacks voted for the first time after the Civil War. But southern states fought to keep them from voting.

"Separate but Equal"

Black Americans were free after the **Civil War**. But they faced a big problem. Many whites still believed that blacks were not as good as other people.

Whites in the South passed **Jim Crow laws**. Jim Crow was the name of a black character from popular plays. Jim Crow laws **segregated** (separated) people. They separated blacks and whites in the South. These laws kept blacks from voting. They kept blacks from holding powerful jobs.

The first "Jim ▶ Crow" was a black character in a play.

Jim Crow laws	laws in the southern U.S. that kept blacks totally separate from whites
segregate	separate

Blacks had to ride on separate train cars, away from whites. They had to use separate bathrooms and drinking fountains. They also had to go to different theaters and schools. Some whites said that black people were "separate but equal." That was untrue, as this photograph below shows.

▼ The dining room for blacks is behind the bathroom.

COLORED DINING ROOM IN REAR

MEN

Ida B. Wells-Barnett's Battle

Blacks tried to fight against **Jim Crow laws**. But they faced deadly enemies. Groups like the Ku Klux Klan often beat or killed blacks. They hurt anyone who did not obey Jim Crow laws. This included white people. Klan members wore hoods and costumes. These hid their faces. It made them look more frightening.

◀ *Ida B. Wells-Barnett fought bravely against lynching.*

Fact!
At least 3,437 people were lynched between 1882 and 1960.

lynch mob   group of people that hurts others
lynching   when a mob (large group of people) kills someone

Whites also formed **lynch mobs**. These were groups of people who hurt others. Lynch mobs killed blacks accused of crimes. Lynch mobs also hurt blacks for no reason at all.

Ida B. Wells-Barnett fought against **lynching**. She worked as a newspaper reporter. Wells-Barnett wrote articles. Her articles raised awareness about lynching. They caused others to join her struggle to stop lynching.

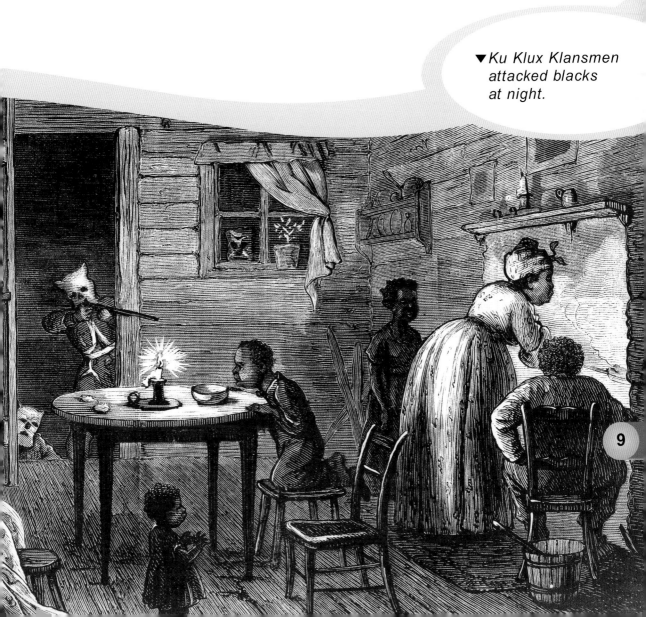

▼ *Ku Klux Klansmen attacked blacks at night.*

9

Changing Attitudes

Imagine seeing ads everywhere that make fun of you. Imagine they show you looking dishonest or lazy.

That is what blacks in the United States used to face. Ads and posters made fun of them. So did plays. White actors dressed up as black people. They acted foolish and silly.

These images made life hard for blacks. Many whites already believed that blacks were not smart or hardworking. Blacks knew that these ideas had to change. Otherwise, whites would never end **segregation**. Blacks and whites would always be seperated.

This NAACP poster ▶ shows a strong, proud black man. It made black people want to join the NAACP.

In 1909 black and white leaders formed the NAACP. This stood for the National Association for the Advancement of **Colored** People. Colored was a common word for blacks then. The NAACP fought against ads that made fun of blacks. The NAACP fought against segregation.

The NAACP was ▼ created to fight anti-black attitudes.

| colored | common word for blacks during the first half of the 1900s |
| segregation | separating people based on differences, such as being black or white |

Jackie Robinson

The Brooklyn Dodgers was a professional baseball team. Their first game of 1947 was on April 15. It was not like most opening days. All eyes were on the player wearing number 42. His name was Jackie Robinson.

Robinson was the first black person to play Major League Baseball in more than 60 years. Black players had been kept out of baseball. Many white players refused to play against them. Instead, blacks had to play in **segregated** (separated) leagues. They had to play in "**Negro** Leagues." (Negro was a common word for blacks then.)

Fans and other players called Robinson names. He even received death threats. But Robinson ignored them. He played so well that the National League named him **Rookie** of the Year.

Both whites and blacks admired Robinson. He showed that black players were as good as white players. He made people wonder why blacks and whites were segregated.

Negro   common word for blacks during the first half of the 1900s
rookie   beginner

▼Jackie Robinson faced many challenges while playing pro baseball.

The 1950s—The Tide Turns

The **U.S. Supreme Court** is the highest court in the country. In 1954 it decided a big **case** that helped blacks. A case is a question or claim to be settled in a court of law. The case was called *Brown v. Board of Education of Topeka, Kansas.*

The Supreme Court said that **segregation** in public schools was not legal. Students could not be separated because of their color.

The NAACP and other groups showed the court photographs of black schools. They proved that black schools always got less money than white schools. So, the Supreme Court said that white schools must **integrate**. They must accept everyone.

This small hut was ▶ a black school near Summerville, South Carolina.

▲ Blacks celebrated the decision in Brown v. Board of Education.

Many schools integrated slowly. Also, theaters and buses were allowed to stay **segregated** (separated).

But the *Brown* case was a big victory for black **civil rights**. Civil Rights are the freedoms all Americans are promised under U.S. laws. They include living wherever you want.

15

case	question or claim to be settled in a court of law
civil rights	freedoms promised to all Americans
integrate	make open to all people
U.S. Supreme Court	highest court of law in the United States

Little Rock

Blacks could finally go to all public schools. But many people in the South still wanted **segregated** (separated) schools. They put up a big fight in Little Rock, Arkansas.

In 1957 nine black students tried to go to classes at Little Rock's Central High School. Orval Faubus was the governor of Arkansas. He told the state's **National Guard** to stop the students. The National Guard is a military unit. It is controlled by each state.

Angry crowds of people showed up at the school. They wanted the National Guard to turn the black students away. Black students had to face the shouting people all alone.

Television news showed images of shouting people. This behavior made people across the country angry. President Dwight D. Eisenhower sent in U.S. Army troops. The army brought back order. The black students were finally allowed to go to Central High.

National Guard military unit controlled by a U.S. state

▼The angry crowds in Little Rock shouted at black students like Elizabeth Eckford.

Rosa Parks

On December 1, 1955, Rosa Parks was riding the bus home. She had just left her job at a store. Parks lived in Montgomery, Alabama.

A white man came on the bus. The bus driver asked Parks to give up her seat for this man. Alabama law said that white people could ask this. But Parks refused. The bus driver called a police officer.

The bus driver asked Parks why she would not stand up. "I don't think I should have to get up," she replied.

The police arrested Parks. This angered blacks in Montgomery. They organized a **boycott** of the city's buses. A boycott means that they all refused to ride the city's buses. The boycott lasted just over a year. A local minister led the boycott. His name was Martin Luther King Jr.

Rosa Parks was ▶ arrested. The police took her fingerprints.

boycott   group's refusal to buy or use something

The boycott worked. The city needed the money from black bus riders. Blacks did not have to give up their seats. Parks was called "the mother of **civil rights**." She helped blacks gain their freedoms.

Free at Last

The number of **civil rights protests** increased during the 1960s. A protest is a way of showing you dislike something.

CORE was part of many of these protests. CORE stands for "Congress of Racial Equality." CORE members believed that protests should not be violent. Members of CORE were forbidden to hit back when attacked.

▼ *Many whites did not want blacks eating at lunch counters.*

▲ *"Freedom riders" faced violence when they protested.*

Many lunch counters in the South would not serve blacks. So, CORE protested. They sat down at the counters. They refused to leave. These "**sit-ins**" made many southern whites angry. Still, the protest worked. Lunch counters were forced to serve blacks.

CORE also held "freedom rides." In some places, blacks had to sit in the back of buses. CORE members refused. Some "freedom riders" were stoned and beaten. One bus was set on fire. But finally the buses changed their unfair rules. Black riders could sit where they liked on buses.

protest   way of publicly showing dislike for something
sit-in   protest in which people sit and refuse to leave

The Children's Crusade

In 1963 blacks in Birmingham, Alabama, could not work at downtown stores. Martin Luther King Jr. worked to change things.

But most blacks in Birmingham were afraid to **protest**. They were afraid to show their dislike in public. The police commissioner made them afraid. His name was Eugene "Bull" Connor. His police often attacked blacks.

King found many children and teenagers who still wanted to help. The children and teenagers marched through Birmingham. They called for change. Bull Connor set police dogs on them. He also turned on fire hoses. Carolyn McKistry was hit by water from a fire hose. She was a high school student.

"It tore a big hole in my sweater and sort of just swiped part of my hair off that side," Carolyn said. *"It was very painful and you couldn't escape."*

crusade   strong effort to achieve a goal

Other Americans saw these images on television. They demanded that Birmingham **integrate** its stores. They wanted the stores open to all people. King's protest in Birmingham was called the "Children's **Crusade**." A crusade is a strong effort to achieve a goal.

▼ Young people were hit by fire hoses in Birmingham's Children's Crusade.

23

"I Have a Dream"

In 1963 public support for **civil rights** was growing. Black leaders like Martin Luther King Jr. pushed the government. They wanted to end the South's **Jim Crow laws**. These laws kept blacks separate from whites. They wanted new laws that gave freedom for all.

Black leaders held a **protest** march in Washington, D.C. More than 250,000 people showed up. Sixty thousand of those people were white. It was the biggest civil rights protest up to that time.

During the march, Martin Luther King Jr. made a speech. He called the speech "I Have a Dream." It was reported in newspapers. It was reported on television. The speech became very famous. This is a part of it:

"I have a dream that one day ... little black boys and black girls will be able to join hands with little white boys and white girls and walk together as sisters and brothers."

▼ Martin Luther King Jr.'s "I Have A Dream" speech became famous all over the world.

Peace prize!

In 1964 Martin Luther King Jr. won the Nobel Peace Prize. It is one of the highest honors in the world. It is given to people who work for world peace.

A New Day

In 1964 the **Civil Rights** Act became law. A year later, the Voting Rights Act became law. Now blacks finally had the same rights as white people. Blacks could vote. No one could stop or bother them. Theaters and hotels could not serve only whites. They could not turn blacks away.

These new laws put an end to the South's **Jim Crow laws**. The Jim Crow laws had kept blacks and whites separate. They had stopped blacks from voting.

Still, some white people did not like the change. They were angry that blacks were now equal to them. In 1968 Martin Luther King Jr. was killed in Memphis, Tennessee. He was shot by a white gunman. King was one of the world's greatest champions for civil rights.

The fight for civil rights continues. Many schools are still divided. Many churches and neighborhoods are divided. Some people still try to **segregate** (separate) themselves. The push for civil rights is not over. It will not end until we all live together in peace.

New laws in the 1960s ▶ allowed blacks to vote in the South.

I Spy

In the early 1960s, there were few black actors on television. The 1965 show *I Spy* changed that. The show had two stars. Robert Culp was white. Bill Cosby was black. They played a pair of U.S. spies. They traveled the world together. They fought the bad guys together.

Before *I Spy*, black actors often had to act dumb or silly to get laughs. But Cosby's character, Alexander Scott, was smart and funny. He got along well with Culp's character, Kelly Robinson. They were a team. Viewers could see that they respected each other.

I Spy was a success. It started a new kind of televison show. Now black and white actors perform together all the time. Nobody thinks twice about it. *I Spy* helped bring **integration** to television.

Bill Cosby and I Spy ▶ *helped make television shows open to all people.*

Glossary

boycott group's refusal to buy or use something

case question or claim to be settled in a court of law

civil rights freedoms promised to all Americans

civil war fight between people from the same country

colored common word for blacks during the first half of the 1900s

crusade strong effort to achieve something

integrate make open to all people

Jim Crow laws laws in the southern United States that kept blacks totally separate from whites

lynch mob group of people that hurts others

lynching when a mob (large group of people) kills someone

National Guard military unit controlled by a U.S. state

Negro common word for blacks during the first half of the 1900s

plantation large farm

protest way of publicly showing dislike for something

rookie beginner

segregate separate

segregation separating people based on differences, such as being black or white

sit-in protest in which people sit and refuse to leave

slave person owned by another person

slavery practice of buying and selling slaves

U.S. Supreme Court highest court of law in the United States

Want to Know More?

Books to read

- Anderson, Michael. *The Civil Rights Movement*. Chicago: Heinemann Library, 2004.
- Levine, Ellen. *Freedom's Children: Young Civil Rights Activists Tell Their Own Stories*. New York: Puffin, 2000.

Websites

- http://memory.loc.gov/ammem/ aaohtml/exhibit/aopart9.html#09a
  Learn more about the struggle for civil rights in the United States at this Library of Congress online exhibit, "The African American Odyssey."
- http://www.cr.nps.gov/nr/travel/ civilrights
  Visit "We Shall Overcome: Historic Places of the Civil Rights Movement," to learn more about important events and places in the struggle for civil rights.

Read **Counting Coup: Customs of the Crow Nation** to find out about the history and traditions of the Crow people.

Read **Rebirth of a People: Harlem Renaissance** to find out about the talented writers, painters, and artists of the Harlem Renaissance.

Index